THEN & NOW

SAGINAW

Opposite: **The Residence of Dr. H. C. Potter, c. 1888.** This home was located at 1404 South Jefferson Avenue. The home was razed in the early 1960s. The Greater Williams Temple Church of God in Christ currently stands on the site.

THEN & NOW

SAGINAW

Kevin Mark Rooker

ISBN 978-0-7385-6119-6

Published by Arcadia Publishing
Charleston, South Carolina

Printed in the United States of America

Then and Now is a registered trademark and is used under license from Salamander Books Limited

Library of Congress Control Number: 2008935192

For all general information contact Arcadia Publishing at:
Telephone 843-853-2070
Fax 843-853-0044
E-mail sales@arcadiapublishing.com
For customer service and orders:
Toll-Free 1-888-313-2665

Visit us on the Internet at www.arcadiapublishing.com

This book is dedicated to my mother, Jacqueline Helena Silkstone, who gave me a love of writing and the joy of photography by encouraging me in both pursuits and never telling me that I could not succeed; to my father, Donald James Rooker, who was always there to lend a hand and his heart when I was in need; and to Bill Ostash for his patience and support during this project.

On the front cover: **GRATIOT COURT AT GRATIOT AVENUE, C. 1925.** The rapid growth of Saginaw resulted in the development of new subdivisions due in large part to the proliferation of the automobile. (Historic photograph courtesy of the Historical Society of Saginaw County, contemporary photograph by Kevin Mark Rooker.)

On the back cover: **PENDELL'S GROCERY STORE, C. 1906.** Pendell's Grocery was located on the curve of the 400 block of East Genesee Avenue. A doctor's office was located up on the second floor. Immediately to the right were two jewelry stores, E. J. Hall and William Stoltz, followed by the William Barie Dry Goods Company. (Courtesy of the Historical Society of Saginaw County.)

Contents

ACKNOWLEDGMENTS

I would like to thank the following people whose help made this book possible: Greg Branch, who answered my questions and pondered over photographs; Saginaw historian Tom Trombley, who willingly researched and gave me invaluable information about photographs sent to him; Curtis Bitman for his development of chapter ideas; Evelyn Mudd and Troy Rhyan for reviewing and editing the text; and the Historical Society of Saginaw County for allowing me access to its photographic archives. Historical society photographs will subsequently be acknowledged with HSSC. All contemporary images were photographed by myself, and unless otherwise noted, all historic images are from my personal collection.

Also consulted while writing this book was *History of Saginaw County, Michigan* by James Cooke Mills, published in 1918.

Introduction

Within these pages one will find that Saginaw was once a city of over 100,000 residents representing just about every ethnic group on the planet. Artists and craftsman poured into Saginaw to work on the magnificent French chateau-styled post office, the Romanesque Hoyt Library, and countless commercial structures and grand mansions. It was a city of industrialists and captains of industry: Wellington R. Burt, Arthur Hill, the Morley brothers, John L. Jackson, and Julius Ippel, among others. As the county seat, Saginaw was the center of an immense agricultural and industrial area.

Saginaw was the lumbering capital of the world in the mid- to late 19th century. As the trees were removed, the landscape was left barren and open. As the lumbering era declined, agriculture and related industries began to replace it. Agriculturally, the area became important in the production of sugar beets, which resulted in spin-off industries such as Spic and Span detergent, now a part of Proctor and Gamble. Saginaw's river port facilities were central to the shipment of grain products.

With the decline of the lumbering era, lumber barons Burt and Hill assisted in the transition to a manufacturing-based economy by building new educational facilities. This helped to prepare a skilled workforce adept at modern manufacturing techniques.

The automobile ushered in a new era for Saginaw with several new foundries and parts plants sprouting up along the Saginaw River. In 1905, the first production automobile, the Ranier, was produced in Saginaw. Automobile pioneer Charles Duryea opened a factory here, as did Marquette Motor Works and General Motors. By the 1920s, it was necessary to recruit labor from throughout the country. The Deep South was a significant source of labor for the automobile industry, and African Americans migrated north in the Great Migration to work in the new factories. During World War II, these automobile plants ceased civilian production and became key manufacturers of wartime materials. Saginaw Steering Gear Plant II was nicknamed "the gun plant" because of the various guns made for the military.

Saginaw is once again in a state of transition as automobile manufacturing has waned. Where once some 20,000 people worked in the various automobile plants along the river, the total is now under 5,000. Today Saginaw is on the cusp of becoming the center of emerging alternative energy industries. In addition, the growth of the medical and health sectors is making Saginaw a renowned regional medical hub.

CHAPTER 1

STREETS AND AVENUES

POTTER STREET. Many of Saginaw's visitors would arrive by train in the late 19th and early 20th centuries. The Pere Marquette Railroad station fronting Potter Street would have been their gateway to a bustling thoroughfare. The lumberjacks coming out of the forests would flock to the many saloons lined up and down this street. Many a lumberjack lost his entire season's pay after a night of drinking and brawling.

LAPEER STREET, GENESEE AVENUE, AND JEFFERSON AVENUE. Considered the center of downtown, the Tower Block stood at the apex of these streets. Adorned with a large clock, copper dome, and imposing statue (supposedly of Jacob Seligman, "Little Jake"), the Tower Block was an imposing edifice. For most of its life it housed offices and a drugstore on the main floor. The large and imposing Schmelzer's (later Feige) Furniture store stood immediately east of it. The Tower Block was razed in an orgy of urban renewal in 1961.

JEFFERSON AVENUE FROM FEDERAL AVENUE. Looking north toward the Tower Block, Jefferson Avenue had some notable businesses located here. The *Saginaw Courier Herald*, predecessor to the *Saginaw News*, was in the building to the immediate right. The large building in the center was Weichmann's Department Store. The only store to have glass-fronted elevators, it occupied the former Avery Building on the corner of East Genesee and Jefferson Avenues. The *Courier Herald* building was razed in order to build the 1931 art deco–styled Peoples Building and Loan.

East Genesee Avenue from Water Street. Looking east toward the intersection of Washington Avenue, this section of Genesee Avenue was particularly busy. Ships would off-load cargo on Water Street for the many businesses downtown. The structures immediately to the left were razed in the 1920s to build the towering Second National Bank. To the right is the Bancroft Hotel, the premier hotel in Saginaw. Seen in the center left is the Eddy Building, which contained offices and shops.

EAST GENESEE AVENUE AT WASHINGTON AVENUE. Looking east, the Eddy Building can be seen immediately to the left where Prall Drugs was once located. In the 1980s, a restaurant opened on the ground floor called Studio Five. It was nicknamed after TV-5 located down the street. It closed in the early 1990s. The line of buildings to the right underwent changes in the 1920s and 1930s. This intersection is the only intersection left in Saginaw where all its buildings are still intact.

Washington Avenue at East Genesee Avenue. Looking north, the Eddy Building can be clearly seen at center right. This intersection was extremely busy, as evidenced by the photograph. Trolleys were the preferred method of getting around town. Owned by the Saginaw Traction Company, they were electrically operated by overhead wires. The building to the far right once was home to WSGW radio, one of the oldest stations in the Saginaw Valley.

EAST GENESEE AVENUE FROM FRANKLIN STREET. The Everett House was another of Saginaw's great hotels. Known throughout the country, it was a favorite of traveling businessmen and lumberjacks. Having electric lights, steam heat, and one of the best restaurants in town, its 65 rooms were nearly always full. Many a lumberjack got his first bath in months here. The hotel was razed, and United Shirt Company built an art deco building. Cunningham Drugs occupied it until the 1970s; WNEM TV-5 remodeled it for use in the 1980s.

FRANKLIN STREET FROM EAST GENESEE AVENUE. The building to the left dates from the 1870s and once was the business location for Brown and Grant Jewelers as well as a men's clothing store. The false facade was put on the building during the art deco craze of the 1920s and 1930s. Note the staircase alongside the building leading to the second floor. The building was last used as a deli in the 1990s. Many of these buildings along Franklin Street were razed in the 1970s and 1980s.

FRANKLIN STREET FROM TUSCOLA STREET. Looking toward East Genesee Avenue, one can clearly see the Everett House in the distant center. The building to the immediate right was home to James S. Smart Jr. and Company, wholesale confectioners. In the 1890s, trolleys would be installed along Franklin Avenue. Much of this block was razed in the 1970s, with WNEM TV-5 now occupying the site of the Everett House.

FRANKLIN STREET. Note the Foresters Temple building on the far left and the Benjamin Franklin Hotel in the center. The Benjamin Franklin was a seven-story brick structure that opened in 1915. It survived the Wright's European Hotel fire of January 1918. Wright's European Hotel stood directly behind the Franklin at 114–116 South Washington Avenue. The Franklin was evacuated but did not catch fire. In 1928, the Franklin did catch fire and resulted in the deaths of two firemen.

FRANKLIN STREET LOOKING NORTH. The Franklin Theatre stood on the corner of Germania Avenue (now Federal Avenue). Opposite the Franklin was the Foresters Temple where the interurban station was located. The interurban trolley system transported passengers between Saginaw, Bay City, Linwood, Bridgeport, and Birch Run. Today the Savoy Bar and Grill operates in the building second from the left. Many of the photographs in this book hang on its walls.

Baum Street from Tuscola Street. This street is not at all recognizable from its 1888 counterpart. Of particular note is the small two-story wood building third from the corner on the right. This typifies the change from frontier town wood buildings to prosperous urban center where businessmen erected brick structures. This entire area was cleared in the 1970s and 1980s with plans to build a downtown mall. When those plans fell through, Baum Street was closed to traffic and the new Hart State Office Building was built at the corner of Baum Street and East Genesee Avenue.

EAST GENESEE AVENUE FROM SECOND STREET. The Boehlke and Elwert wallpaper store stood at 819 East Genesee Avenue. Specializing in window coverings, paint, and wallpaper, it was a prominent store in 1888. Notice the very large gas streetlight on the sidewalk. Only prosperous businessmen could afford this kind of technology, which was sporadic in the city. The Tower Block is visible in the distance before its clock, copper dome, or statue were installed. Many of the buildings were razed during the 1970s and 1980s.

East Genesee Avenue Looking West. The William Barie Dry Goods Company can be seen immediately to the left. This large enterprise was a fixture in downtown Saginaw for decades. It was built by the Germania Society on land willed to it by Anton Schmitz. By the 1960s, Montgomery Ward would occupy the building. In the next block, Seitners and Peoples Savings Bank are located. The tower of the Heavenrich Department Store can be seen on the right. (Courtesy of the HSSC.)

East Genesee Avenue at Warren Avenue. Parson's Business College occupied a stately three-story brick building known as the Dunk Block, which was built in 1887. The college also had a location in Lansing. On the ground floor was Greyes Picture Store, specializing in frames and artwork. At the far end of the block is the white Avery Building. Eventually this would become Weichmann's Department Store. The entire block was razed in the 1980s using urban renewal block grant money.

COURT STREET FROM HAMILTON STREET. The R. J. Birney Company occupied the corner of Court and Hamilton Streets. Specializing in medicines, paints, stationery, and the like, stores such as this carried a wide array of products in order to capture sales. This building would eventually be replaced by the gleaming white terra-cotta structure of the Bank of Saginaw, which later became Second National Bank. Today City Finance Mortgage Company operates in the building. The tower of the fire station can be seen in the distance.

HAMILTON STREET AT COURT STREET. Looking north on Hamilton Street, Bauer Clothing House was located in a thriving business district. It was a men's store specializing in gents' hats, coats, and other furnishings. The courthouse stood only a block away, and many savvy lawyers of the day bought their suits from Bauer. By the early 20th century, Bauer Brothers had expanded beyond men's clothing, selling mostly home furnishings. This entire block was demolished to build a city parking deck in the 1970s.

Hamilton Street at Van Buren Street. By 1888, most frontier-styled wood structures had been replaced with stately brick buildings. J. H. Benjamin opened a carriage factory on this corner to provide transportation for the increasing population of Saginaw. His Concord Buggies were of the highest quality and known throughout the Saginaw Valley. His factory building is now a collection of shops and a jewelry store.

CHAPTER 2

Grandness in Granite and Brick

Fordney Hotel. Situated on the southwest corner of Hamilton and Court Streets, the Fordney Hotel was one of Saginaw's preeminent hotels. Originally the Taylor House, the Fordney was named in honor of Joseph Fordney, who spearheaded an effort by the West Side Business Association to purchase and renovate the run-down Taylor House, which had been built on the site of Old Fort Saginaw in 1866. In 1909, it reopened as the new Fordney Hotel. A massive fire consumed the building as well as three other buildings in 1991.

MICHIGAN SUGAR COMPANY. Michigan Sugar Company sits not far from the river on a major railroad line in the community of Carrollton. The factory is perfectly situated to take advantage of transportation networks and the abundance of sugar beets grown in the rich soils of the Saginaw Valley. The plant has undergone numerous expansions over the years and currently is not processing beets due to the high cost of its oil-fired boilers. Future plans call for its reutilization.

MICHIGAN BEAN COMPANY. Located on Niagara Street on the west side of the Saginaw River, Michigan Bean Company was originally Producers Elevator Company, a grain elevator. Albert L. Riedel, who guided the transition to Michigan Bean Company, was instrumental in the creation of the Jack Rabbit logo and neon sign. The elevator building itself is the largest bean elevator in the world. The operating neon bean bunny is 35 feet tall and 50 feet long, making it the largest figural neon sign in the United States.

Herzog Art Furniture Company. Begun in 1909 by John Herzog, the Herzog Art Furniture Company was located at 1909–2000 South Michigan Avenue. The massive structure was built of brick sandstone and produced fancy desks, tables, and music cabinets. Most of the fine furniture was made of mahogany and caught the attention of the Sonora Phonograph Company of New York, which merged with Herzog in 1923 when radio cabinets were in high demand. Unfortunately for Saginaw, the parent company in New York gained complete control in 1929 and went bankrupt in 1930.

Modart Corset Company. Opened in 1909 on a different site as the LaFrance Corset Company, Modart was a leading employer and manufacturer of ladies' undergarments. The four-story brick building was built in 1920 on the corner of Lapeer and Second Streets by J. Fred Beckbissinger, a prominent local architect. Shortly after the building's construction, employment soared to over 300 workers, making upwards of 7,000 dozen garments per year. Today Corset Shop Intimates of Saginaw has its roots in Modart, as it started out as a company store within the factory building at Lapeer and Second Streets. (Courtesy of the HSSC.)

HOTEL VINCENT. Located on the corner of Washington and Federal (once Germania) Avenues, the Vincent was a five-story brick building constructed in 1890 by James Vincent and lumber baron Arthur Hill. It was one of the most beautiful hotels in Michigan and was furnished with only the best; private baths, beautiful wall coverings and ceilings, and electric lighting highlighted the elegant building.

BANCROFT HOTEL. Located on the corner of East Genesee and Washington Avenues, the Bancroft Hotel was the premier hotel in Saginaw. Originally built in 1858 by Jesse Hoyt as a four-story structure, it was razed in 1915 to make way for a newer, grander hotel. Built at a cost of $500,000, the Bancroft Hotel contained 237 rooms and a lobby featuring huge panels of American walnut. The first incandescent bulb in Michigan lit the Bancroft Hotel. This view is from Water Street at the foot of the Genesee Street Bridge.

BENJAMIN LIVERY STABLE AND UNDERTAKER. C. L. Benjamin began his livery business by providing storage, wagons, and buggies to individuals and businessmen. Eventually he offered the use of horse-drawn hearses to local undertakers, one of whom set up business in an adjoining office. His son, M. I. Benjamin, expanded the business further by constructing a beautiful brick structure on the corner of Cass Street and Hamilton Street. Today the building is the home of the Stable, a bicycle and sports shop. The undertaker's display cases, built of oak, walnut, and pine, still exist on the second floor. (Courtesy of Rachael Louise Walsh.)

SCHUST BAKING COMPANY. Henry Schust had this building constructed at the foot of Congress Street on Michigan Avenue adjacent to the Michigan Central Railroad tracks. Designed by Cowles and Mutscheller, renowned Saginaw architects, the building stands five stories tall and cost $100,000 to build in 1915. The bakery made biscuits, crackers, and cookies and sold them as far away as Chicago. Henry died in 1933, leaving the operation of the bakery to his sons, Emanuel, Edward, and Gustav. The company was eventually acquired by Sunshine Biscuit Company, which moved operations out of Saginaw. Art Sample Furniture occupies the building today. (Courtesy of the HSSC.)

AVERY BUILDING. Located at the southeast corner of East Genesee and Jefferson Avenues, the Avery Building was a two-story white brick building. In 1888, Schirmer Brothers Jewelry Store occupied the building. The building was eventually razed, and a much larger structure was built in its place. The larger structure would be occupied by Weichmann's Department Store. In 1888, it was common for many businesses to hang clocks outside their stores for the convenience of the shopping public.

Weichmann/Avery Building. The Avery Building became known as the Weichmann Building as soon as the William C. Weichmann Company moved into the building. The store boasted glass-fronted elevators and a beautiful mezzanine where the fine china department was located. With the construction of Fashion Square Mall in 1972, Weichmann's moved its store to the mall, ending decades of presence in downtown. Weichmann's ceased operations in 1993. The downtown location was razed in the early 1980s.

MORLEY BROTHERS HARDWARE. In 1863, Edward and George Morley joined Anton Schmitz in the hardware business. By 1880, the Morley brothers were the largest hardware wholesalers in Michigan; by 1892, they were the second largest in the nation. In 1882, a 100,000-square-foot building was constructed on North Washington Avenue and expanded again in 1927. The Morley family chartered Second National Bank (now Citizens Bank) and loaned Billy Durant, the founder of General Motors, working capital for his new company. Their store window displays during the holiday season were a sight to behold. Morley's ceased retail operations in the early 1980s, and its flagship store was razed in 1981. (Courtesy of the HSSC.)

HEAVENRICH BROTHERS DEPARTMENT STORE. Founded by Max Heavenrich and his brothers in 1886, the store occupied the former Seligman Building located on the corner of Franklin Street and East Genesee Avenue. In the 1920s, a newer building was constructed. It boasted large display windows and a second-floor mezzanine as well as elevators. Max Heavenrich died in 1953, and operation of the store passed to his son. Heavenrich vacated its downtown location with the construction of Fashion Square Mall and eventually went out of business in the late 1980s.

FRUEH FLORIST. Charles Frueh came to Saginaw from Germany in 1872 with training in floriculture. In 1875, he built his first greenhouse on Hoyt Avenue between Walnut Street and Genesee Avenue. The storefront pictured here was built in the middle of the block between Emily Street and Park Avenue surrounded by greenhouses. By 1912, the business had outgrown the space on Hoyt and was moved to Genesee Avenue and Webber Street while the storefront moved to 514 Genesee Avenue. Frueh died in June 1914 while picking roses in his greenhouses. (Courtesy of the HSSC.)

EDDY BUILDING. Erected as the Crouse Building around 1872, the Eddy Building is one of the last buildings in downtown Saginaw that dates from the time Saginaw was the lumber capital of the world. Most of that era's buildings were razed during the urban renewal craze of the 1970s, 1980s, and 1990s. Prall's Drug Store occupied the ground floor for decades, while the upper floors housed doctors' and lawyers' offices. Currently the Eddy Building is being used as a rent-subsidized apartment building.

Saginaw State Bank. Located on the corner of Jefferson and East Genesee Avenues, this building eventually became known as Michigan National Bank, under whose ownership the building was greatly enlarged to include the first drive-through bank windows in the city. Michigan National Bank continued to operate in the downtown area until the late 1990s, when it was acquired by Standard Federal Bank, now Bank of America. The building is now the main offices for Health Delivery Inc. (Courtesy of the HSSC.)

Consumers Power/Bank of Saginaw. Lumber baron Myron Butman was one of the principal organizers of the Bank of Saginaw and served as its president for many years. Absorbed by Second National Bank (now Citizens Bank), the building was purchased by Sears, Roebuck and Company, which greatly altered the structure. Today it is home to the Saginaw Police Department. Located at Federal and Warren Avenues, Consumers Power Company had its main office only a few blocks from its central steam plant. Lieberman Trunk Company occupied the building from the 1950s through the 1970s.

SAGINAW NEWS BUILDING. Located at the corner of Federal and South Washington Avenues, the current Saginaw News is the descendant of several other Saginaw publications. One of these, the Saginaw Courier Herald was originally located in the 100 block of South Jefferson Avenue. Growth necessitated a move to a larger, more modern facility. The new structure was full of large windows and clad in gleaming white stone with lions' heads between each arch. Growth once again forced the Saginaw News to build an even larger facility next door in the 1950s.

Hamilton Block. The Hamilton Block was a large three-story brick building fronting on East Genesee and South Jefferson Avenues. Hamilton's Drug Store was a growing concern in the 1880s, selling medicines, bandages, and supportive clothing. Competition was fierce in Saginaw between the many drugstores, often more than one on every block. Bruske Drug Store lured customers by selling a relatively new delight, ice cream, as can be seen in this 1888 photograph. This block was razed in the 1970s.

FRANKLIN THEATRE. Built in 1914 at a cost of $120,000 by a group of South Jefferson Avenue businessmen, the fireproof Franklin Theatre was located at 132 Franklin Street on the corner of Federal Avenue. Vaudeville performances were the mainstay of the theater until the advent of motion pictures. The building then underwent renovations to improve the acoustics and install a large screen, remaining in operation until 1973. The building was razed a short time later. (Courtesy of the HSSC.)

Temple Theater. Built in 1927 by the Elf Khurafeh Shriners on Washington Avenue, the Temple Theater is the largest theater in Michigan outside Detroit. Butterfield Theaters leased the building and operated it through the 1970s. Originally opened as a vaudeville and silent movie house, the theater served as Saginaw's premier movie house for many years. With the demise of the downtown, the theater fell to hard times and neglect, only to be restored at considerable cost by the Shaheen family. It currently serves as a center for Saginaw's cultural events. (Courtesy of the HSSC.)

STANDARD OIL BUILDING. The Standard Oil building stood at 230 South Washington Avenue on the corner of Janes Avenue. The music academy originally stood on this site but caught fire and burned in 1917. The first oil field discovered in Michigan was in Deindorfer Woods in the summer of 1925, which got the attention of Standard Oil Company. The company built its main office in downtown Saginaw and built a series of small gas stations throughout the city. Today the site is occupied by Spicer Engineering Group in a building constructed by AT&T. (Courtesy of the HSSC.)

CHAPTER 3

RELIGION, EDUCATION, AND PUBLIC LIFE

ARBEITER HALL. Arbeiter Hall was one of a handful of magnificent buildings constructed in the 1880s and was built by the German Workingmens Association. This association assisted sick members with a payment of $5 per week for up to 26 weeks. It would also assist with funeral expenses of $50. The association bought land located at Janes Avenue and Fourth Street and built a three-story brick structure at a cost of $20,000. In 1912, it was reported that the Saginaw association had over 600 members, the second highest in the state. The building no longer stands on the site.

ARMORY BUILDING. The armory building is a late Gothic Revival structure built of Saginaw brick in 1909 that faced Water Street on the corner of Janes Avenue. The Saginaw Auditorium sat directly behind the armory on Washington Avenue. The three-story building once was the home of the 2nd Division of the Michigan State Naval Brigade and later Company B, 1st Battalion, 125th Infantry of the National Guard. It was vacated in 1982 and sat empty and deteriorating until extensive restoration began in 2003. It is now available for office and retail space.

Castle Post Office. Built in 1897 by the federal government for use as the city's post office, the building occupies half a city block bounded by Federal, Warren, and Jefferson Avenues. The "castle" was made to resemble a French château in order to honor the French explorers who discovered this area for Europeans. With Saginaw's rapid growth, the post office needed to be expanded, and it was rebuilt and enlarged in 1937. Facing possible demolition in the 1970s, the Saginaw County Historical Society purchased the building, and it now houses the historical museum.

JEFFERS FOUNTAIN AND PARK. Bounded by Genesee, Federal, and Warren Avenues and one block from the center of the downtown business district, this small park was created by John Jeffers and his niece Elizabeth Champe. John Jeffers had the fountain and bust of his brother Michael Jeffers built in 1906. Michael Jeffers was an entrepreneur and philanthropist, responsible for building many downtown structures. The fountain's plumbing passes through a large vault where blocks of ice would be placed in order to cool the water. The fountain and park are being restored to their 1906 condition.

Hoyt Library, Castle Building, and Baptist Church. This view is looking north on Jefferson Avenue from Janes Street. Hoyt Library was built in 1887 and opened fully in 1895. Built in the Richardson Romanesque style, it is composed of limestone and Lake Superior red sandstone. An expansion was done in the 1920s, and the Janes Avenue entrance was created as a replica of the entrance to Canterbury Cathedral. The Baptist church in the distance was demolished to make way for the art deco Peoples Building and Loan in 1931.

Saginaw City Hall. Located on the entire city block bounded by Remington Avenue, Holland Avenue, Water Street, and South Washington Avenue, the original city hall was an imposing structure. Standing five stories tall, it was built of brick and stone in 1893. When the city of East Saginaw and Saginaw City combined in 1889, it was agreed that the courthouse would remain where it was on the west side and the new city hall would be located on the east side but one mile between the two city centers. A disastrous fire in 1935 completely destroyed the building and a smaller art deco building was built on the site. (Courtesy of the HSSC.)

SAGINAW COUNTY COURTHOUSE. The courthouse was built on the corner of South Michigan Avenue and Court Street in 1884. The center portion of the structure was substantially enlarged late in the second decade of the 20th century by adding the north and south wings. The needs of the county would again outgrow the building, and in 1969, county voters approved a plan to replace the structure with a "modern" building. Construction of the new courthouse took place behind the old courthouse, which was razed in 1972. The four-sided clock was saved and installed in a new clock tower on the front lawn.

St. Mary's Hospital. This five-story brick hospital was built in 1892 after outgrowing its original location, the Monitor House located at 623 North Washington Avenue. The Daughters of Charity, along with Fr. Francis van der Bom, opened it in 1874. During those first few years, St. Mary's Hospital offered the first-of-its-kind health insurance in the nation. The hospital's closest brush with disaster was the great fire of 1893 that swept across 23 blocks from Holland Avenue to Emerson Street. The brick structure was one of only a few that survived the fire. The building was expanded in 1960 and again in 1982.

WATER TREATMENT PLANT. Located on Ezra Rust Drive, this magnificent stone-and-brick structure was built in 1929 to safely treat river water and pipe it to people's homes. Water pumps on street corners supplied water to residents not connected to the waterworks system. However, brackish water in the aquifers below and increasing pollution of the river made obtaining a safer source necessary. A 65-mile pipeline was constructed from Lake Huron at White Stone Point in 1948. This pipeline is jointly owned with the City of Midland. Saginaw consistently has some of the highest-quality water in the United States. (Courtesy of the HSSC.)

EASTSIDE HIGH SCHOOL. The Eastside High School was located on Warren Avenue in the 400 block on the corner of Millard Street. The school was built in 1865 when Saginaw was in the midst of the lumber boom. Most boys were off working in the lumber camps and related industries; thus, more girls attended the school. The building no longer exists, and the site is now occupied as a Saginaw School District storage facility.

Burt Manual Training School. Situated opposite Eastside High School on Warren Avenue, the manual training school was built by Wellington R. Burt in 1904. Burt, a lumber baron, was one of the wealthiest men in the country and realized the lumber era was nearing its conclusion and the jobs that came with it were fading. He knew there was a need for training and education in new industries. The facility, built at a cost of $750,000, boasted the best in modern equipment. A swimming pool with a South Weadock Avenue entrance was opened in 1905. The building was razed by the board of education in the 1980s.

Hoyt School. Located on the corner of Hoyt Avenue and South Jefferson Avenue and large by the standards of the day, the length of Hoyt School covered half the block between Hoyt and Emerson Street. Built in 1871–1872, it replaced the old academy that stood on the same site and burned in 1871. Originally only six classrooms for 325 students, in 1892 it was expanded in order to accommodate 400 students. A parking lot for St. Mary's Hospital occupies the site where Hoyt School stood.

EMERSON SCHOOL. Emerson School stood on the corner of Emily, Merrill, and Mott Streets in East Saginaw. The original Emerson School was a small brick structure of four rooms built in 1872. The need for a larger school became apparent with Saginaw's increasing population. A two-story building sporting a bell tower was built on the site. The school was again replaced with a more modern structure in the 1960s.

First Congregational Church. The First Congregational Church is located on the corner of Jefferson Avenue and Hayden Street in what was the center of a rapidly growing neighborhood and city. Immediately surrounding the church are the magnificent mansions of Saginaw's lumber barons and businessmen, yet only a street away are more modest homes of its working class. Designed by architect Gordon W. Lloyd of Windsor, Ontario, and built by C. S. Chapin of Buffalo, New York, it was begun in 1866 and opened in June 1868. It is an ornate building of solid red brick in the Italianate style. A disastrous fire in 1973 destroyed the roof, but the Tiffany and other stained-glass windows were saved.

St. Mary Cathedral. Founded in 1853, this is the third building constructed for the parish on the same site. St. Mary Cathedral, located at 601 Hoyt Avenue, was erected in 1901 and dedicated in 1903. Built in the Gothic style of Saginaw paving brick and limestone, the structure is massive and elegantly proportioned. The interior was heavily remodeled in the 1970s, removing much of the historic components, and the slate roof was replaced with asphalt shingles. Plans are currently underway to restore these architectural features.

Academy of Music. The Academy of Music stood on the corner of Janes and Washington Avenues. Built in 1884 by investors William L. Webber, James B. Peter, and Wellington R. Burt at a cost of $70,000, it was 70 feet across by 140 feet long. Designed by architect J. M. Wood of Chicago, it was said that the academy was the "finest theater in the state" at the time. The Academy of Music exemplified the change from frontier town in the 1850s to the bustling city it was in the 1880s and 1890s. The academy was consumed in a fire on April 17, 1917. Standard Oil Company would eventually build on the site.

MASONIC TEMPLE. Located on the corner of Johnson Street and North Washington Avenue, the Masonic temple was a five-story redbrick-and-stone building. The massive structure, built in 1856, cost an astounding $175,000 ($4.375 million in 2008 dollars). The auditorium had seating for 1,200, and the entire building was lit by gas, a luxury at the time. The building was demolished when the Saginaw Civic Center (now the Dow Event Center) was built in 1971.

SAGINAW AUDITORIUM. The auditorium was built by lumber baron Wellington R. Burt on the site of the former Simpson Grocery Store in 1908. Located on the corner of Janes and South Washington Avenues, the auditorium could seat an astounding 4,000 people. Burt left several provisions for the building's maintenance or expansion; a trust was set up to maintain the building in perpetuity if at least two walls of the structure were left standing, thus allowing for remodeling or expansion. When the civic center was built, city leaders felt there was no need for the auditorium, and it was summarily razed in 1972, thereby returning the trust funds to the Burt estate.

YMCA. This Saginaw YMCA was the second building to be erected in Saginaw for the organization. The first was located in downtown Saginaw on the corner of Tuscola and Franklin Streets. The building seen here was constructed in 1912 on the corner of Michigan Avenue and Ames Street. The wills of both Arthur Hill and Aaron T. Bliss made provisions for its construction. As Saginaw's population grew, an even larger YMCA was proposed. A new $3 million structure opened in 1960 on the banks of the Saginaw River and Fordney Street. (Courtesy of the HSSC.)

ELKS CLUB. This two-story building was located on the corner of Warren and Federal Avenues with an entrance on both streets. Made of brick and stone, the building was constructed in 1906 on land purchased for $5,000. Most structures at the time, including most homes, had shallow basements; thus, the building appears to have an extra half story. The drive-through lanes for the now-closed bank stand on the site.

CHAPTER 4

HOME AND HEARTH

THE CORNING MANSION. At the north end of the Grove District at 1446 South Washington Avenue stands one of the most impressive homes ever constructed in Saginaw. It was built as a duplex for T. B. Corning and his son in 1872. Filled with splendid stained-glass windows, marble fireplaces, and massive furniture, the house was turned into a home for the aged in 1920 according to the wishes of the Cornings. The home has undergone extensive restoration and is now a single-family residence. (Courtesy of the HSSC.)

SCHMELZER MANSION. John Schmelzer built his magnificent home in the Grove District in 1892 at a cost of $25,000 ($581,395 in 2008 dollars). Designed by architect Clarence L. Cowles, the home had Ionic columns inside and out. Mahogany wainscoting, beamed ceilings, parquet floors, marble fireplaces, and crystal chandeliers graced the interior. Schmelzer was one of the first to own an automobile, and he purchased an electric car, which was stored in the carriage house along with its charger. The home was purchased by the city in 1961 and razed in the mid-1970s. Schmelzer died in 1947 and is buried in Calvary Cemetery. (Courtesy of the HSSC.)

SCHUETTE MANSION. Built in 1874 by William H. Clark, this home is located at 1537 South Washington Avenue in the Grove District. Clark owned a dry goods store in East Saginaw. By 1898, lumber company owner William Schuette had purchased the home when he arrived here from Pittsburgh. He was an associate of the Mershon, Schuette and Parker Lumber Company. He and his wife Florence did not stay in Saginaw long, as they moved to New York in 1908. The home has a large dining room with a special alcove for musicians. Much of the home is paneled in fine woods, with an elegant fireplace tucked away in the library. (Courtesy of the HSSC.)

JEFFERSON AVENUE. This photograph is looking north on Jefferson Avenue from Hayden Street. Jefferson Avenue was the center of the social scene of East Saginaw. The mansions of lumber barons and Saginaw businessmen lined Jefferson Avenue for blocks. The towering steeple of Grace United Methodist Church (formerly Jefferson Avenue United Methodist Church) looms above the homes below. Its steeple was toppled by a storm in 1896 and rebuilt on a smaller scale in 1987. Many homes had carriage steps and hitching posts along the street.

Webber Mansion. This magnificent mansion and its grounds occupied half a city block, surrounded by a wrought iron fence. William L. Webber, attorney for Jesse Hoyt, bought and finished the home started by Chester B. Jones. Sitting on Millard Street between South Warren Avenue and Sheridan Avenue, the home was an imposing edifice. Built of brick and stone with 18-inch walls and a tower that stood 65 feet high, the home was the most magnificent residential structure in Saginaw. Pres. William Howard Taft and other dignitaries were entertained here. In 1961, the Saginaw Board of Education decided to build administrative offices on the property and the home was demolished.

Hoyt Avenue. This 1888 view of Hoyt Avenue at South Warren Avenue is located several blocks from the central business district of East Saginaw. The neighborhood became home to many of Saginaw's powerful businessmen and civic leaders. Jesse Hoyt's brother Alfred built a Gothic-styled home here along with the Wolfarth, Draper, and Waltz families, to name a few. Many of the homes were of mansion caliber, but there were also more restrained homes mixed among them.

WOLFARTH HOUSE. Frank W. Wolfarth, a prominent Saginaw baker, built Wolfarth House in 1893. He owned the largest steam bakery in the state of Michigan. Four fireplaces, massive oak staircases, and gas lighting grace the home. Daughter Leona, upon her parents' deaths in the 1930s, acquired the home. She sold the bakery to a Detroit firm, which went bankrupt during the waning days of the Great Depression. Leona died in 1973, passing the home to her nephew Frank Wolfarth Walsh. Walsh fought to save the home when it was slated for demolition by the local school district for a parking lot. He succeeded, and preservation-minded individuals bought the home in 1992, completely restoring it.

GERMAIN MANSION. The Germain mansion was located at 1571 South Washington Avenue in the Grove District. Built in 1893 by Edward Germain at a cost of $30,000 ($714,285 in 2008 dollars), the home had 20 rooms with a two-level reception hall sporting open galleries on three sides. Meant to resemble a great English baronial hall, it had an ornately carved main staircase. Each room contained a different kind of wood: mahogany, cherry, walnut, and oak. Nine fireplaces graced the home, and the third floor had a finished ballroom where the Germains entertained often. (Courtesy of the HSSC.)

ARTHUR HILL MANSION. This stately home was built on the corner of Michigan Avenue and Remington Avenue (formerly Bristol Street) by lumberman Arthur Hill. Constructed of brick and stone, the home was impressive yet unpretentious. Born in 1847, Hill moved to Saginaw and traveled the timberlands for his father. Eventually he formed his own company and became very profitable. Seeing that the Michigan forests were running out, he extended his landholdings into Minnesota, Canada, and the Pacific Northwest. Sadly, the home caught fire and burned. The Saginaw Art Museum annex stands on the site.

Court Street. Now part of the Heritage Square Historic District, this portion of Court Street was the center of a thriving residential district in the early 20th century. Most of the homes here were of wood-frame, clapboard construction. Large and stately, these were the homes of Saginaw City's movers and shakers, many of whom owned businesses in the district near the county courthouse. Many of these fine homes fell to the wrecking ball in the 1970s, while others were converted for law offices. (Courtesy of the HSSC.)

North Michigan Avenue. This neighborhood was considered one of the most desirable in which to live. These were the homes of Saginaw City's wealthy and famous. Arthur Hill's residence was only a block to the right in this photograph, along with the Ring Mansion. This particular image records the removal of the trolley lines and pouring of concrete fill in the mid-1930s. Many of these stately homes were razed for office and commercial space during the 1970s and 1980s. (Courtesy of the HSSC.)

ADAMS BOULEVARD. This residential neighborhood was created during the heyday that was the Roaring Twenties. Saginaw was in the middle of an automotive manufacturing boom, and the population was growing rapidly. Subdivisions were sprouting up around the perimeter of the old neighborhoods. These homes were built around 1925. The automobile enabled people to live farther from the city center and not rely on the trolley system for transportation. Homes built at this time were more modest in scale when compared with their early-20th-century counterparts. (Courtesy of the HSSC.)

GARDEN LANE. Located just south of Gratiot Avenue, Garden Lane was another neighborhood developed during the Roaring Twenties. Originally part of lumberman Ammi Willard Wright's land holdings, the homes are modest in size as well as in materials used. Most of the homes of this period were wood clapboard as opposed to brick and stone. These homes were built around 1927 and reflect the emerging importance of the automobile, with each home sporting a driveway and small garage. (Courtesy of the HSSC.)

STATE STREET. This section of State Street was beyond the reach of the Saginaw Traction Company trolley system. Built one and a half miles from the city center, these emerging neighborhoods depended more on the automobile than the electric trolley system. They also reflect the purchasing power of the middle class as more and more people worked in the automotive industries that made up much of Saginaw's industrial base. (Courtesy of the HSSC.)

CHAPTER 5

Green Gold and the Iron Horse

Washington Avenue Looking Southwest. The lumbering industry was in its heyday in the mid-1880s. At the peak of production Saginaw boasted nearly 50 sawmills operating along the banks of the Saginaw River. The riverfront was smoky and dirty and crowded with sawmills, docks, and railroad tracks. Docks extending into the river enabled schooners and barges to load lumber bound for Chicago and other Midwest destinations. The waterfront was the lifeblood of the community and its most dangerous arena. Spinning saw blades, moving logs, and machinery without regulation posed constant threats to sawmill workers and lumberjacks.

Lapeer Street at Second Street. In 1888, the lumbering industry had begun its decline. The various industries that thrived on lumbering continued to prosper and would for another 20 years. There were no zoning codes in those days, and it was not unusual for a mill or factory to be in a neighborhood of houses. Lapeer Street was a heavily commercialized area with small shops, small industries, and residences combined. It also led directly into the center of downtown, some four blocks away. The Tower Block can be seen in the middle of the 1888 photograph.

Pere Marquette Court Street Depot. This depot served Saginaw City before the consolidation with East Saginaw. Set back from Court Street some 100 feet, it sat perpendicular to Court and parallel to Woodbridge Street about where the apartment building currently sits. The curve of the railroad bed can still be seen today. Fifty-two trains arrived and departed Saginaw, carrying passengers and freight to other Michigan cities. Passenger service ended in 1962, and this depot was demolished in the late 1960s.

MICHIGAN CENTRAL RAILROAD STATION. Located near the intersection of North Michigan and West Genesee Avenues behind the present-day Walgreens drugstore. Situated about 300 feet off and perpendicular to Genesee, the station was beautifully proportioned of stone and red brick. An imposing tower stood on the northeast corner of the building. This was the location of the last passenger train to service Saginaw in 1962. The station was razed in the early 1970s.

PERE MARQUETTE RAILROAD STATION. The Pere Marquette Railroad station is one of the last grand Victorian stations in the country. Designed in the Romanesque style by architect Bradford Lee Gilbert, it was built for the Flint and Pere Marquette Railroad. A separate power building located to the east of the main structure provided heat. Approximately eight sets of tracks sprawled out in front of the depot at the height of its activity where only four exist today. In 1990, a group of concerned citizens formed the Saginaw Depot Preservation Corporation and purchased the depot. A tragic fire on April 16–17, 1991, destroyed the depot's expansive roof and badly damaged the second story. The spectacular tower collapsed shortly after the roof was replaced. Plans are underway to replace the tower as well as continue restoration work.

Downtown Saginaw Riverfront Docks. The riverfront along Water Street was a busy part of the city in 1906. Docks for passenger disembarkation as well as cargo and freight stretched along the riverfront from Genesee Avenue to Bristol Street (now Remington Avenue). Visible in the photograph is the top story of the music academy on the far left as well as the roof of the armory and auditorium at center left.

SAGINAW CITY RIVERFRONT. In 1888, the riverfront along Niagara Street in Saginaw City was lined with lumber docks and sawmills. The Michigan Central Railroad and others had direct access to the lumber docks with tracks laid between them and Niagara Street. Salt production was at its peak with barrels loaded on barges and shipped to ports throughout the Great Lakes.

A. W. Wright Lumber Dock. Ammi Willard Wright (1822–1912) came to Saginaw in 1851 at the age of 29 and set out prospecting lands along the Cass, Flint, and Tittabawassee Rivers. His choosing of some of the finest timberlands around Saginaw made him a fortune. He founded several companies and acquired and merged others until he incorporated A. W. Wright Lumber Company in 1882. The company comprised huge holdings of timberlands, railroads, lumber properties, sawmills, salt blocks, and lumberyards. These immense lumber docks located on the west bank of the river north of Bristol Street (now Remington Avenue) were a testament to his business acumen.

Lumber Docks and Holding Pens. These lumber docks were located north of the Genesee Street Bridge along the west side of the Saginaw River. Logs were floated downriver and sorted by identifying the log mark of the owner. Logs of the same owner were rafted together and sent on to be captured at the owner's sawmill. At this lumber dock can be seen the log boom holding area, sawmill in the background, and processed lumber sitting on the docks ready for shipment.

EDDY LUMBER DOCKS. Charles K. Eddy (1820–1901) came to Saginaw in 1865 and involved himself in the lumber business. In 1880, he purchased the old Chicago Mill. Remodeling, enlarging, and adding new machinery, Eddy was able to cut and ship 18–20 million feet of lumber. Located south and at the west end of the Genesee Street Bridge, the mill site also contained a salt block. This block used brine from four wells producing 50,000 barrels a year. The mill was disassembled when the lumbering era came to an end. The concrete retaining wall was built by the Eddy sons while cleaning up the lumber mill site.

James H. Pearson Lumber Mill. In 1865, James H. Pearson of Chicago became a business partner with Ammi Willard Wright in the A. W. Wright and Company lumber firm. The mill burned, but a larger, more sophisticated mill was immediately built on the same site. A large planing mill was built downriver near Bristol Street (now Remington Avenue). In 1871, Pearson retired from the firm of A. W. Wright and Company and built a large mill of his own along Niagara Street on the west side of the Saginaw River.